THE BEST PROJECT MANAGER

A booster to enhance your Power Skills in 2023

Prabuddhi Sattrukalsinghe
(MSc Project Management, PMP, CSM,
PgD Business Psychology)

Foreword

Project management has evolved from an expeditor and coordination role to the management of complex pieces, from system conception to design, integration, delivery, and long-term support.

Along the way, methodologies, processes, and tools have been developed which, with the help of computer technology, have enabled improved planning, tracking, and control.

This book is different, it is about the Key Power Skills required to execute a project successfully in a collaborative approach. This book focuses on the important elements of power skills, alongside management and leadership and on the careful balance between them in a project management environment. Much more importantly and uniquely, this book is a guide for achieving excellence as a Project Manager.

During my career, I have worked with many Project Managers who could have benefited from the advice offered in this book. Indeed, I met one outstanding Project Manager during my many roles in the Aviation front, and I was always aware that there was little written about leadership in project management.

For this reason, I was pleased when Prabuddhi asked me to help review drafts as she made progress with the book. While I contributed little to the messages in the book, I did become confident that the world of project management and business in general, would be much better served because of the guidance in this book.

Prabuddhi has done an excellent job of capturing all her thoughts pertaining to management and leadership - thoughts that she has garnered over the course of her career. She presents them, and a practical model, as a framework of the important components that lead to personal excellence in project management. I witnessed her excellent power skills in executing complex projects.

Furthermore, Prabuddhi presents a self-evaluation guide to measure one's progress toward personal project management excellence. This is unique and will be of interest to seasoned Project Managers, people transitioning to project management, and those who are just starting a career in project management. Indeed, it will also be of interest to those who have general business management roles.

Kishore Ganesh

Aviation Executive.

Contents

Foreword 1

Introduction 4

Are you one of them? 5

Why now? 8

DEEP 9

DEEP Understanding 10

D - Diagnose 10

E- Establish 11

E- Evolve 11

P- Pursue 12

An example of a Good Project Manager 12

DEEP Power Skills 15

Diagnose: Innovative Mindset 15

Diagnose: Problem Solving 19

Diagnose: Accountability 23

Establish: Communication 26

Establish: Collaborative Leadership 34

Evolve: Strategic Thinking 37

Pursue: Relationship Building 40

Review 44

What makes a unique project manager? 48

References 49

Introduction

You may be an expert in project management, or an amateur to this field, no matter what your current state is, I assure you that you will benefit from this read.

By the end of this book, you will notice that there is profound depth in project management skill requirements other than the famous areas of creating project charters, planning, budgeting, scoping, executing, risk management, etc.

In this book, my focus is on "Power Skills" that makes the unique character of a project manager who strives to be successful through collaborative leadership.

According to PMI's latest research, it is identified that if project managers are to be successful in their career, they need to possess these skills and master them. You will learn 7 major Power Skills under an introductory model called DEEP.

First, we **d**iagnose what we need and how we need to apply them, followed by **e**stablishing what is required, and **e**volving to continue and **p**ursue these skills.

I hope you revel in the read and will be able to relate to your experience as this is a practical guide aiming to make you better at what you do and a little push for you to become The Best Project Manager you ever knew in your life.

Are you one of them?

When I say, "Best Project Manager" I am not looking at well-known project managers like Henry Gantt, Imhotep, Ustad Ahmad Lahori, or Lu Youmei.

Not surprisingly, we can say they were brilliant by looking at what they achieved. However, my focus here is for us to disburse into a more sophisticated view of a project manager's must have skillset through which they can become 'The Best' at what they do.

How do we know we are doing our best? Think... Think....

Here are some clues to know if you are at your best while wearing your Project Manager hat. Take a good look at them as you will need these while you keep reading till the end for you to better understand the correlation of Power Skills we are reviewing about.

You *consider yourself as a business partner in your organization.*

You *get compliments about your email writing style and the way you facilitate meetings and presentations.*

You are praised (if not, you are self-aware) about your ability to come up with solutions and adapt rapidly when uncertainties pop-out as if they were some corn kernels that were stuck in a heated pressure cooker (that moment when you attend a meeting and boom! There is a risk highlighted about the vendor's resource unavailability...)

You are not reluctant to give credit to your team members when its due and it doesn't seem like a left-handed compliment.

Your interaction with your team goes beyond the daily-stand-up meeting, they feel connected, and you confidently rely on them for the tasks assigned to them.

You consider your stakeholder updates are a necessity and not a milestone that you just need to tick mark for the week.

You love change. Change in requirements, change in processes, change in environment, change in market, change in qualifications, change in technology...

You are not rattled when uncertainties arise.

You do not get demotivated when things do not go as planned.

You believe in integrity and accountability.

For some of us, this may seem unrealistic, while some others are reaping the best out of their positions as Project Managers using simple but effective ways in which they make this happen consistently. Attention! I said, *"consistently"*. This should be your aim.

Why now?

In this current time, we all know that technical skills alone will not favour project success. According to PMI Pulse of the Profession - 2023, Power Skills (Interpersonal/Soft skills) are the key to Project Success as it is necessary to have that higher level of influence to achieve a common vision. If you notice, PMI has even updated the Talent Triangle. "Technical project management" is replaced with "Ways of Working", "leadership" is replaced with "Power Skills" and "Strategic and Business Management" is replaced with "Business Acumen".

Higher the rate of project failure, deeper the research has gone into identifying the actual root cause/s of failure. As a matter of fact, the research and further details of PMI's Talent Triangle update can be found in Narrowing the Talent Gap where it states that there is a need for 25 Million project professionals by the year 2030 to close the talent gap. We as project managers will need to focus more on strategic leadership behaviours if we are to survive and thrive for the best.

DEEP

From this chapter onwards, I am going to introduce you to a model, and I named it as **DEEP**. Yes, its DEEP. What we need to understand is Deep. Surface level perception will not help you to become the best.

In my 15 years of career, in which the second part purely focused on Project Management, I discovered simple but effective ways to ensure I am an effective leader who is able to manage a team, deliver a product on time and have peace of mind without having to explain myself to superiors over and over again due missed deadlines, unmet quality standards, conflicts with stakeholders and all other chaos that comes with projects.

Nonetheless, achieving this state is not easy, you need a lot of analysis, emotional intelligence, exposure to different project environments, cultural awareness, diversified teams and above all, you have to make sure you are playing to your strengths and not allowing your weaknesses to dominate.

(Note: Get in touch with us if you would like to know more about your strengths and weaknesses via www.fortiorintel.com).

DEEP Understanding

We as project managers need to be active in both hemispheres of our brains. At times we need to seek knowledge, gather experience, ideas, logics and on the other hand we need to be able to produce innovations, solve complex problems through creative thinking skills. Our minds should be accustomed to see beyond what the naked eye can see.

Let's see what we are about to reveal in the upcoming chapters through this introductory model called "DEEP".

D - Diagnose

In this chapter, you will learn about 3 Power Skills that are considered as essential for a successful project manager and why those are important. Author will trigger your thinking to self-assess your skills and analyse the current behaviours to see if you are on the right track. You can then go deeper to understand the areas of improvements that are suggested through prompts along with questions to make your own plan. You will diagnose,

- Innovative Mindset
- Problem Solving
- Accountability

E- Establish

Once you have diagnosed the areas under Innovative Mindset, Problem Solving skills and Accountability, author will then consider establishing your communication skills to be effective in all aspects as a project manager.

A detailed review on effective communication and its application in real project management scenarios are explained which is followed by guidelines on establishing Collaborative Leadership. You will establish,

- ➢ Communication skills
- ➢ Collaborative Leadership skills

E- Evolve

After a thorough review and understanding on areas to work on, the next chapter elaborates the importance of Strategic Thinking and how you, as a project manager should evolve from your current state to step-up to the challenge and become the best version of you. You will evolve in your,

- ➢ Strategic Thinking.

P- Pursue

Finally, after all the skills are diagnosed, established, and then evolved to be implemented, the Project Manager is not to be stagnated in one place, they need to keep pursuing their skills. The key to pursuing the skills and keep improving is to keep pursuing the relationship building skill. This is a skill that needs to be continuously reviewed, observed, and improved. Hence, in this chapter you will be guided to pursue your,

> ➢ Relationship Building skills.

An example of a Good Project Manager

I recently came across a great real-life example to elaborate the significance of the skills that we are going to explore under DEEP model.

It is next to impossible to find someone who does not watch Netflix these days. Have you watched the reality Netflix series called "Dream Home Make Over"? I just loved this show for many reasons at the beginning as it resonates with my love for home interior, and the way she makes other people's dreams come true, it's so satisfying to see. But, when I reached season 3 of the series, it was a *bright shoot* as I began to be more observant about her Project Management skillset. I was mind-blown.

My learnings when Shea meets her clients to understand requirements at first – Requirement gathering.

1. Clarity in understanding the client requirement/s with minute details that would create the WOW moment.

2. Active listening, paying attention to every little detail.

3. Questions focusing on better clarity to avoid working with assumptions and surprise!

4. Building client trust from step one.

My Learnings when she heads back to discuss with her team – Project Planning.

1. You are nothing without your team, respect their inputs and incorporate them. If you do, you will have a team that is connected and dedicated to deliver your vision.

2. Check for your team's capacity and only then, agree to the timelines. This way, you don't overpromise to client and stress your team.

3. No information is hidden, the team is aware of what to do and what not to do, how to stay within the budget, as she makes them feel part of the project and their views are taken into consideration.

When the work is in-progress – Project Execution.

1. You have to be fully engaged with your people, not by looking at progress reports and charts while sitting at your office, sipping coffee. This is how you get to deliver what you promised.

2. Change is certain. Accept it and be creative. Your job is to find solutions, not to go whining to everyone about how difficult your job is.

3. Do not get rattled when things do not happen the way you expected.

You may find more real-life examples if you pay attention to detail in what you see, shared above to give you a hint on the skills that are practical and applicable to bring out best outcomes from our efforts.

DEEP Power Skills

Well, let's see if you can remember the clues I gave you in our first chapter, to understand if you are at your best. There is a connection between those clues, Shea's example and the 7 power skills that we are about to explore.

These skills were identified through the PMI survey carried out and demonstrated in PMI Pulse of the Profession - 2023. However, in this book, I have categorized these under our preliminary model "DEEP" for better visualization and connection.

Diagnose. → **E**stablish. → **E**volve. → **P**ursue.

Diagnose: Innovative Mindset

For a project manager, having an innovative mindset doesn't necessarily mean that you are an idea generator of new concepts and business designs. For us, it means that we are able to come up with solutions to most unexpected situations. We have to be creative and exclusive. That's what makes us special.

Having said that, it is also wise to note, when you are a project manager, your creativity cannot just be based on imaginations and assumptions, it has to be based on numbers, data, previous lessons learnt, trends, probabilities, etc. Why do I say that? Well, you may have either experienced or seen how important it is to understand the probable outcome of an action when you are dealing with projects. You may encounter situations where alternate options are required to achieve the end-goal, but can you risk your budget ? timelines? Do you have the tools? Is it against the protocol? Do you have the skillset within your team? Is it breaching any security clauses? Has anyone done this before? these are some of the questions that you need to ask yourself before jumping into conclude the alternate.

How do you nurture this behaviour?

> **Train your mind to be analytical** .

   Have fun while gaining some skills. If you think you are not much of an analytical thinker, try engaging in Crossword Puzzles, Logic Puzzles, Riddles etc.

   Research shows that exercising more can bring in more cognitive ability as well. So, there you go, you can kill two birds with one stone.

   Ask questions, don't shy away!

   Read more often.

- **Join groups and communities.** You are not alone. If you explore the groups and communities that are available in social media channels such as LinkedIn, Twitter, Reddit, Quora, you will be surprised with the number of questions, discussions that hover around some of the similar problems you have. This is a great way for you to gain more knowledge, ideas and some of the industry tricks that are tried and tested. One piece of advice here, don't frame your circle to only "project managers", spread your wings and explore other areas like, technology, education, psychology, emotional intelligence, body language, etc.

- **Practice applying 3 W's and 1 H to problems you solve.**

Don't worry about how people are going to think of you if you seem to ask questions to clarify requirements more often. Make it a first priority at any given situation to ask yourself (or others if required) these questions,

Who is your target customer *(you should be aware of what they like, dislike, what will satisfy them and what will trigger them).* Remember how Shea asks questions before she takes on a project?

Why do they need this *(remember to always make sure you are addressing their primary requirements. You*

cannot change the requirement in case if you had to provide alternate creative solutions during the project).

What are those instances that customer is planning to use this product or service? *(You should be well aware of the product or service usage areas. Yes, you! Not the business analyst. Make sure you are on top of this game).*

How are they going to use this? *(Have a holistic view of the planned product launch, target audience of the client, product usage trends, competitors).*

What are we trying to achieve here? An innovative mindset that puts analysis into practice for informative decision making to find creative solutions in unexpected situations. Read that again.

So, start diagnosing yourself just like how your GP would do when you go to get some flu medicine. Remember, you visit the GP when your over-the-counter medicine doesn't respond, which suggests that this is in fact Deep and needs actual diagnosis. Ask yourself questions. Did your family members have anger issues? were there anyone who was absentminded?. I am just teasing, reminding you of your GP's style of questioning.

Questions to self	Yes | No | Maybe	If not "YES", what's my plan?
Do I keep myself updated with latest business knowledge in my area of work?		
Do I check for available data from all possible resources to base my decisions?		
Do I make sure that my client's requirements are crystal clear to me and my team?		
Do I support change?		
Do I see unexpected situations as opportunities?		
Do I respect others' opinions when finding solutions?		

Diagnose: Problem Solving

Well, having a creative idea will be of no use if you have no clue how to apply that to bring about a workable solution. If you have been successful in identifying a problem, congratulations! You are halfway there.

Most managers, scrum masters, project teams fail when they are unaware of problems that are sitting inside the project due to lack of attention to detail and being just stuck inside their own bubble, no time to analyse the progress and probable risks, just going with the flow. No, that's not how best project managers and teams' work. They make sure that they are hands-on with all the details of the project and continuous analysis is carried out.

Business analyst's job doesn't end when the user stories are uploaded, they continue to work checking on the requirements, will the client look for any alternates, review negative flows, discussions with other stakeholders and continuous reviews to understand the project is on track. Quality analysts work doesn't start when the product is released for review, it starts when the development starts, they work alongside development team by giving their insights, reviewing the user stories along the way, comparing, and providing feedback to the team.

That's how the project managers and their teams identify problems before it occurs and come up with workable solutions. If you have not analysed the details, worked as a team, forget about identifying it or solving it, you may create a greater mess.

Check point!

Try to answer these questions honestly, and by the end of this book, review your answers. I hope you will make use of some self-realization.

1. If your team has business analysts, how do they gather requirements? If not, who is gathering the requirements?

2. What is the technique they are using to gather these requirements? Do you get actively involved?

3. Is it robotic? Or feels more connected to the stakeholder who is requesting the product?

4. Does your business analyst team support throughout the project by looking into minute details and what other possibilities and alternates that are/will be available in the market by the time you are ready to launch your product?

5. Is it only the quality analysts who are checking the quality of your development? And when do they do that?

6. Do you have the habit of sharing information about the project with your team transparently or do you feel you are more powerful when you have this information exclusively for yourself?

7. Do you actually get engaged with your team to discuss the progress and practice active listening?

8. Do you facilitate reviews with stakeholders who will actually use the product or launch the product?

9. Do you encourage change before it's too late based on your knowledge and up to date demands on the competitive market?

10. Do you initiate discussions with stakeholders when you think they need to be aware of certain changes and information on the project or do you wait until your next scheduled meeting to discuss the matter?

Remember, you are your doctor here. Act like a surgeon now, not just a GP. Run some scans and tests. Ask the question, answer yourself, prescribe the medicine with the help of guidelines given above. I am instigating your thinking through these questions, answers are already included in the questions, pay attention, and think deeper.

What are we trying to achieve here? A project manager who is aiming to solve problems by practicing prevention over treatment. If you see the 10 questions above, and decide to practice more engagement, you will create and lead a team who is well organized and engaged in every step of the way, preventing issues before it occurs.

Diagnose: Accountability

PMI defines Accountability as "taking psychological ownership for what you say you will do" (PMI Pulse of the Profession - 2023).

Imagine if you were to work with a bunch of people who take responsibility for what they commit. If you like what you are envisioning, start with yourself. Make sure you keep your word when you commit to something. Think twice, pause, and think again before you commit, if you do, you have to bite the bullet.

Now take a moment to revisit what you have committed so far in that one project you were given, or the multiple projects where you had to gamble your time around. How many times did you commit to your team that you would sit with them to review and clarify a requirement at a particular time and then you completely missed it without even taking time to inform the team? How many times did you tell your product owner that you will look for other options to suit their requirement and you will get back to him/her within an hour and then you wondered what was the requirement just before the next scheduled review? By consistently failing to meet your plans with the team and client/product owner, you will lose their trust in you, they will no longer be comfortable in speaking to you about their issues, they will not see you as a leader who can support them in time of need.

These may sound tiny little things, but they make a huge impact. Don't forget we are first dealing with people, then comes the project output. You first need to understand and connect with your people to be successful in your project.

How often you had actually submitted a report before the client requested it? If you did, you deserve a pat on the back, because the impression you make about your accountability and responsibility to your client is beyond excellence. This builds trust, they feel they can rely on you and that they do not have to supervise your work, you will take on their role in the project making sure their requirements are delivered as per expectations. However, if you are the opposite of this where the client has to always remind you or wait for the weekly/monthly reviews to understand some important issues, risks, mitigation plans etc., you are not really making a good impression, in fact you will keep them on their toes every time they see your name as the "project manager" on their project.

It is you who decides whether you are the best at what you do or not, so take lead and invest time in yourself to first understand your ways of working. Review, revisit and adjust.

By now, after *diagnosing* these three skills, i.e., Innovative mindset, problem solving and accountability, I hope you are able to identify your strengths and weaknesses in these areas and that I have provided some insights for you to go back to the drawing board.

In the next chapter we will see what you need to *Establish* in order to become better at what you do as a project manager, scrum master, team lead, product owner, or any other fancy name that your organization may have given you.

Establish: Communication

They say haste makes waste. I hope you have not rushed through our chapter on diagnosing your skills that are most desirable to be the best version of yourself. If you took your time to read and explore other connected areas, you may have been enlightened more about how well you do your role and what are your strong and weak points. I hope you made some notes.

Once you have thoroughly reviewed your current status, it is time to now establish what is required to get better. Let's start with your communication skills.

> "Effective communication is 20% what you know and 80% how you feel about what you know",
> Jim Rohn.

I couldn't agree more here, because we are not talking about just communication, we are in the business of "effective communication".

What good it would do to you if you felt like you were barking up the wrong tree each time you tried to pitch a project proposal? Or if you just had to bite off more than you can chew simply because you didn't really know your way around your sponsor to give you approval for the extension you requested?

For your communication to be effective, you need more than just language skills. Yes, I agree the language skills are required, but that alone would not get you where you want to be. Then what would?

Next, you will see 22 other factors that contributes for your communication to be effective.

(Tip: count the number of letters in these two words).

EFFECTIVE COMMUNICATION

Energetic : Be energetic when you arrive at work, greet your team (don't keep a frowning face), make sure you are in control of the energy that you operate in. Positivity will start flowing.

Fluent: Be absolutely sure of what you are talking about, presenting, commenting. Do not leave room for someone to doubt your level of understanding. Take precautions if you need to improve on some areas.

First-hand: You are the lead, you need to be the first to know, first to inform, first to table it for discussion. This shows that you are in control of what you are doing.

Empathetic: This is not new. You know it. If you don't understand the other person's point of view, you will not be able to satisfy your client, sponsors, team members. So, pull your socks and take steps to practice active listening, emotional intelligence, body language, and read more about these topics to keep yourself updated.

Creative: Don't be boring when you facilitate meetings, presenting project progress. Create your own style where people wait to see you at meetings. Prepare beforehand, not in the last 15 minutes of your presentation, please!

Timely: Nobody gets excited with stale-news. Know your game, be updated about what is relevant to your project and be ahead of your competitors. Do not think it is the job of your marketing manager to inform your project sponsors or clients about the market trends that are relevant to your product or project. Take lead in every possible area, and you will not regret it.

Informative: Being informative doesn't necessarily mean that you always need to write paragraphs in emails and use all possible infographics in presentations. This means that you need to be on top of the game by knowing all details related to your project, and when you present, speak, discuss, you need to be confident enough to answer or clarify any questions asked.

Value-added: Be it a casual discussion with your team, your colleague, sponsors, anyone that is in your project or even a different project, if you are speaking, make sure you are adding some value. If not, nobody cares about your opinion and your past experience or any fancy story that you might like to share. So, if you are not adding value to the conversation, step back.

Easy-to-comprehend: Don't sound like a "Sheldon" when you present or speak. People do not have time to praise your intellect. If you are presenting or reviewing something with your team, sponsors, and other stakeholders, get to the point and make it easier for them to understand, so you can get the best out of your meeting time without having to waste more time in explaining via emails and one-on-one telephonic conversations afterwards.

Cultural fit: You need to understand as a project manager, you should be a total package of all goodness. The way you dress, the language you use, your body language when you sit for meetings, it all needs to be thought through. You gain respect by respecting other people, so don't forget to start from yourself, pay attention and make an effort.

Openness: This should be your motto. You are expected to be open about the project with all stakeholders, including the sponsor. No hiding business. Transparency is the key. You are not to hide details from your team nor from other stakeholders. Be on alert and be open to speak, be open to constructive feedback, take courage to present the real picture, but don't just land there with no solutions. Bosses don't like managers who doesn't have solutions as they have bigger fish to fry.

Meekness: Being kind doesn't cost a thing. In fact, you will gain more because of it, it will help you to generate that positive energy I spoke about in the first point (being energetic). Be kind to those who come to you with problems, questions, ideas. Show that you care, genuinely. Don't fake it. Make an effort, and you will get there (*mean it, don't keep looking at your phone or laptop screen when your teammate is speaking to you, that's first of all annoying and secondly, shows how much you care*).

Mindfulness: Humans don't feel safe to work with people who sound or looks like they are completely lost. We look for security in places we work. So, if you are not being mindful about what you do, what you speak, it will be evident to others. Pay attention to detail, be updated, do not wait until someone comes to you and give you updates about the project that you are leading, you need to be the person who is getting the information first-hand.

Uniqueness: Do not try to copy anyone, be yourself and people would love to work with you, communicate with you. Be humble, create your own image where others can see a difference that encourages valuable conversations with you, be the figure of a leader without a title, you do not need a title to lead, you just need some genuine effort.

Numbers: Believe me, if you don't know your numbers, you will embarrass yourself in front of others, sponsors, clients. You got to be good with what is happening with your budget, capacities, estimates, dates, deliverables, backlogs, etc. It may not be easy for you to answer from top of your head if suddenly a question is asked at a meeting if you don't have the habit of going over your facts and numbers first thing in the morning when you start your day. This builds confidence and you will see how confidently you can speak when you know your numbers.

Impactful: Everyday, make it a habit to review what you have done, understand if you were successful in creating an impact. It doesn't always have to be a steering committee meeting or a status meeting, it may be a simple conversation, but that goes a long way if you did manage to make an impact with your inputs. Practice it consciously.

Confident: Be confident about your ability and skillset. Do not hesitate to speak the truth, table your opinions. Your sponsors, your managers, stakeholders all are dependent on you for the successful delivery of your project, so take the chance and lead the way. Create that charismatic power and make it visible.

Accountable: Look before you leap. If you promise something or commit to a delivery, achieving a milestone, do what you got to do to make it happen. Check regularly to ensure you are on track, do not depend on anyone else to keep that check, you know it best. If you come across a challenge, do not wait until the date of the milestone to speak about it, you are required to discuss and mitigate it and keep up with your word. Don't let others create labels for you that doesn't add value to your resume.

Team-centric: Take it with a grain of salt. You are not a magician to do it all by yourself. Your team is your strength, give them the credit for what they are achieving. Ensure you speak highly about them with your sponsors, stakeholders, and make sure their work is displayed diligently. They will adore you for that, because everyone is here to make their lives better, whoever supports that will be admired.

Integrity: Be honest to yourself first. If you know you have a risk that is hindering the project timelines, speak up. If you know that you are unable to achieve the target of a release date due to resource unavailability, ask for help, do not wait until the next scheduled meeting to discuss such things, it doesn't show that you are being honest with the situations if you do so.

Observant: Be observant of you surrounding, your teammates, colleagues. There may be other projects that are running in parallel in the organization that may directly impact your project, and if you are not observant enough, you might be inviting trouble at a later stage of the project. However, do not forget, you also need to be observant about the product that your team is building too, it is not only the quality analysts' job to make sure they are delivering a quality product. You need to get connected, communicate and be on alert.

Nudge: Remember how you send that "nudge" when you need attention? Bring that nudge with you when you present, speak, or negotiate. You need to have your audience attracted to you for all the good reasons and that has to do with your ability to take lead as a project manager, the skillset you have mastered. They need to feel that you are in fact the leader. No one wants to hear that you were waiting for some updates from a third party, or you were waiting to get some feedback from your colleague as it definitely doesn't sound like you are owning the project. You need to be ahead of time and gather all required information before you go for meetings and discussions. No one likes to hear things that doesn't make sense or boring.

Establish: Collaborative Leadership

If you are a project manager, you cannot be a person who prefers to work in silo, which means, you should not be feeling strong when you work in silo. You should realise that more you let your team collaborate and work together, better the outcome is going to be and you as the leader, should initiate activities to encourage this collaboration.

Easy does it. Take a moment to revisit how your daily/weekly/monthly meetings are conducted.

Ask yourself these questions,

1. Do I speak more or listen more?

2. Do I let others speak or do I interrupt them habitually?

3. Do I always give the solutions to situations based on my understanding and the background work I carryout, or do I discuss with my team transparently to understand their views?

4. Do I prefer to always take lead in the meetings, or do I let my team members who are experts in their areas to also pitch in and take lead when it is necessary?

5. Do I encourage my team to discuss amongst themselves when looking for solutions or do I encourage them to come up with their own ideas and solutions and reward them?

It sounds basic, isn't it? But go deeper in your thinking when answering these. Think of the possibilities based on your actions and how it would change if you did otherwise in case if you think you can do better to initiate collaboration.

Here are some benefits you can aim to reap if you encourage collaboration.

> **Innovative problem solving**

Come up with solutions with a combined expertise rather than just one person's knowledge and experience.

Ownership and accountability as a team builds trust and bonding.

Positive employee engagement

When employees are engaged to contribute to a vision that is clear to them and sees the alignment to organizational goals, they feel content, and they tend to work with a purpose.

When they are appreciated and they have a chance to enjoy their work, employee retention rate goes up.

High engagement reveals the skillset of your team, which allows you to place them in the correct role based on their strengths.

> **High productivity**

Engaged employees take ownership of their work and it is unnecessary to micromanage them.

They believe they are the experts in what they do, hence they produce to best outcome with nil to minimum supervision.

When the right talent is placed at the right place, you can expect the best out of them rather than pushing them to do things they are not good at.

TIP: You will understand how to succeed if you study failure. Pay attention when teams are not performing well, find the root cause. Do not take a rain check on your analysis to understand root cause when things go wrong. Make sure you cut the mustard when identifying the root cause and avoid creating a storm in a teacup as it doesn't do good to your work atmosphere.

Evolve: Strategic Thinking

Remember my first clue to becoming best at what you do? "You consider yourself as a business partner in your organization". What do business partners do? They look for opportunities everywhere to get better as a business, their job is to create value for the organization.

Same goes for us, project managers. What do we do by initiating a project? we thrive to make a change of the current status of the organization to get better and land in a different status (positively). We see a gap in the market, we propose a project, we deliver it to make sure we gain competitive advantage. We create that value for the business by creating a unique product or service and get ahead of our competitors.

The ball is in your court, if you take lead in initiating such progress or not is up to you. But, if you do, you are clearly a strategic thinker as you seek to align with your organization's goals. You will not be stagnated in one place until you retire if you are this kind of person, because you certainly add value to the business and that is what any business leadership will admire as this is also seen as future-focused orientation which is a skill recognized to be important to succeed as a project manager in the PMI research that I was talking about earlier in the previous chapters.

Through our discussions above, we understand that Strategic Thinking includes, analytical skills, communication skills, problem solving and the overall management skills. However, I am going to give few tips to further understand and improve your strategic thinking if you think you are still on your way up there.

1. Start asking strategic questions, the type of questions that provoke innovative outcomes, however, ensure the answers are supported with facts. Key to strategic thinking is to have your ideas, concepts supported with data and facts.

2. Reflect and observe to understand the path your organization is taking in alignment with their published goals.

3. Do your research on disruptive competitors.

4. Understand the purpose of every product and service that your organization is offering, then match them with the goal.

5. Analyse processes. If you find any gaps, question, discuss and look for possible opportunities to close them.

6. Do not work with assumptions. Conduct interviews with subject matter experts, get into discussions to find more in-depth details to leverage your decision making.

7. Question your own ideas to help you identify your weaknesses pre-emptively and ensure you are not ignoring any possibilities with better opportunities.

8. Do not ever stop learning and making yourself available for formal training to develop yourself.

Now, take a step back. You learned in the diagnose section about three skills, i.e., innovative mindset, problem solving and accountability. If you are to evolve in your strategic thinking, you need to first master these three skills. Then, see how we incorporated about establishing communication and collaborative leadership. Seeing an opportunity, then identifying a solution is the first step, but if you are to be successful in launching this as a project, you need to be able to win this proposal and find a sponsor.

To do that, you need to work collaboratively and make every effort to communicate the proposal effectively to gain approval to move forward. That's the thought process I am trying to plant in you through this model "DEEP". Do you agree that this is in fact deep and just surface level analysis and thinking will not get you there?

Pursue: Relationship Building

This is our backbone and at times it is hard to wrap our heads around this, simply because this is to do with people. People are complicated, but it's not rocket science if you genuinely make an effort.

Let's look at the areas in which we have to deal with relationship building when we run projects.

- Getting started with a project.
- Gathering requirements.
- Procurement.
- Development.
- Internal and external approvals.
- Internal and external testing.
- End user feedback.

Essentially, from start till end and even after the project is released, we need to build relationships and you cannot put an end to it. That is the sole reason why I am describing this under our "pursue" section.

I did mention in our first chapter that as project managers, we have to survive and thrive to become the best. So, being able to create healthy relationships at every touchpoint in your project is the key for you to be able to survive the moment and thrive for the best.

In my experience, I found it helpful to make relationships with people when I tried to understand their ways of working, preferences, and their styles. I am sure you may also be doing intensive exercises in building your stakeholder analysis and matrix to give you an overview of how things should be managed in terms of communicating with your stakeholders and how often you have to have meetings etc. That's all good, however, I am going to give you a bonus piece of information as I have mastered this skill and thought it would help you as well in terms of relationship building, especially with your team and amongst your team.

In 2020, I was introduced to a theory when I was studying for my master's degree in project management (it was new to me, however not so new to the world as it existed from 1970's). This was about "Belbin's Team Role Theory". At that time, I just read through and used it in my assignment, didn't really know the actual details of how the theory can be applied in many areas. In 2021, I decided to take this further, and I got myself accredited to be a consultant of Belbin's Team Role Theory. It was astonishing to see how well we can work with our teams, stakeholders, when we know their styles and preferred ways of working.

Here is the theory in a nutshell. Dr. Meredith Belbin invented this theory where he identified 9 different Team Roles in which everyone of us operates in a work environment. Then he also provided details on their preferred working styles based on their strengths and weaknesses. These are identified through a series of assessments that are done on each individual, which also includes feedback from their colleagues, managers, etc. So, it is not just your view about your skills, it is how others see your strengths at workplace. There are different types of reports to make use of if we want to identify our team's compatibility, our working relationships etc. A Team Report and a Working Relationship report can be used to identify skill gaps, manage conflicts, re-shuffle talent to remove skill gaps.

This process can even start from recruitment, where we recruit right talent for the project. In this case, there is an assessment done with the hiring manager to understand the job requirements and then match the candidates appropriately, so you end up having the perfectly suited candidate and a perfect combination of skills for the project you intend to launch.

The nine roles are as follows. Plant, Resource Investigator, Implementor, Shaper, Coordinator, Team Worker, Specialist, Completer Finisher and Monitor evaluator. You can visit our website, www.fortiorintel.com to read more about the theory and its usage. There is a lot we can do with this information, and we can create more engaging teams for better relationships and project outcomes.

Best part, imagine if you knew the preferred style of your co-workers, project members, sponsors, how easy it would be to handle their expectations? You do not necessarily have to run assessments on all of them, but if you at least do this with your team, you will get an idea and then you can work around using the concept and details.

This will most certainly allow you to manage your project relationships effectively without having to be in disguise at times when you meet new clients, or land at a new workplace.

Review

Now that you have gone through the chapters of Diagnose, Establish, Evolve and Pursue, let's glance over the first 10 clues I shared to understand their connection to these Power Skills we discussed.

"You consider yourself as a business partner in your organization".

If you are able to mark this as a "yes", you are practicing **Strategic Thinking.** If you are not there yet, start using the hints to improve yourself. Remember what business partners do...?

"You get compliments about your email writing style and the way you facilitate meetings and presentations".

Are you comfortable in marking a "yes" here? Go back to our chapter to review the insights on **Effective Communication.** Review and reflect to see where you need to adjust. Remember it is not just the language skills.

"You are praised (if not, you are self-aware) about your ability to come up with solutions and adapt rapidly when uncertainties pop-out as if they were some corn kernels that were stuck in a heated pressure cooker (that moment when you attend a meeting and boom! There is a risk highlighted about the vendor's resource unavailability...)"

If you are not there yet, make plan, keep a target date to review again and work on your plan. Start tracking your progress. Take few minutes every day to understand how you feel at work, when do you feel most strong, keep a journal so you know where you are heading. I hope you will get there soon. If you are already there, congratulations on your **Problem-Solving** skills. Keep rocking.

*"**You** are not reluctant to give credit to your team members when its due and it doesn't seem like a left-handed compliment".*

I am sure most of you would be able to mark this as a "yes". In case if you are struggling, read more about leadership, understand the characteristics of different leadership styles and identify yours. Once you have done that, you will be able to see where you need to improve, because if you do not currently know your style, you might not be able to improve. Remember to always understand the root-cause and apply the fix, just as how we do in projects. This way you will improve on your **Communication and Collaborative Leadership** skills.

*"**Your** interaction with your team goes beyond the daily-stand-up meeting, they feel connected, and you confidently rely on them for the tasks assigned to them."*

By now you have understood how **Effective Communication** plays a critical role in a project manager's life and how you should be supporting **Collaborative Leadership** to gain the best outcomes from your projects. Make it a lifestyle, how you communicate, how you pay attention to yours and other's body language, practice active listening mindfully.

*"**You** consider your stakeholder updates are a necessity and not a milestone that you just need to tick mark for the week".*

Remember you are a business partner. You take ownership, you take lead, you show **Integrity** and **Accountability,** so your clients rely on you wholeheartedly. You will not wait for your client to initiate discussions because you are the one in-charge, and you are in control of all situations pertaining to your project/s.

*"**You** love change. Change in requirements, change in processes, change in environment, change in market, change in qualifications, change in technology..."*

Change is the only constant and you need to embrace it as a project manager. One moment you cannot harp around and say you practice agile, when in the next moment you reject client requirements simply because that was not in the plan. **Innovative Mindset** will attract ideas, allow change, support improvement and welcome creative thinkers and will not feel threatened when surrounded by likeminded people.

*"**You** are not rattled when uncertainties arise."*

You are the leader that your team is looking up to. You cannot afford to lose that trust they have in you. Be mindful of every moment, practice patience, analytical and **Strategic Thinking** is what will reward you with immense **Problem-Solving** skills.

*"**You** do not get demotivated when things do not go as planned".*

Nothing good comes easy and where is the fun if it is all easy and not challenging? If you don't have puzzles to solve in your work, come up with mind-blowing solutions and ideas as a team, you will lose interest in your role. Hence, practice **Collaborative Leadership** and you will enjoy your work along with your team when the going gets tough.

*"**You** believe in integrity and accountability".*

How successful you are by the end of a project, throughout the project, after the project, is all dependent on how good your relationship is/was with your team, stakeholders, sponsors, vendors and everyone around you. How satisfied and content you are is the ultimate measurement of your success after completing a project, and for that you should be on top of the game in **Relationship building,** which is the glue that combines all other Power Skills you learnt so far.

I hope I was able to give you a little push in taking that step towards success in your career. Look at the last page to see a summary of unique characteristics of a Powerful Project Manager who can in fact call themselves proudly as "Best in the industry".

Stay focused! Happy Project Management!

What makes a unique project manager?

1. Easily approachable, welcomes change, appreciate technology.

2. Works as part of the leadership team in his/her organization and considers every opportunity to bring in value to business and processes.

3. Communicates effectively through active listening, positive body language, empathy, and high emotional intelligence.

4. Fluent in the context of their speech in terms of data, numbers, market research, latest technology, competitor analysis and focus groups.

5. Encourages collaboration and supports their team to be engaged in achieving the organizational goal.

6. Able to wear different leadership hats according to the need of the hour. A servant leader when the team requires support, a visionary leader when the team requires guidance and clarity, and majority of the time behaves as a coach and a pacesetter.

7. Highly regarded by the leadership for their persuasive power.

8. Shows charismatic power in their interactions with their own teams as well as all other stakeholders involved in their projects.

9. Consistent in behaviours that they have adopted to be the best in their field and does not fluctuate depending on situations as their approaches are more composed and decisions are more informative.

10. Technically savvy, values professional education and values continuous learning.

References

Pulse of the profession® 2023, 14th edition | PMI. Available at: https://www.pmi.org/learning/thought-leadership/pulse/power-skills-redefining-project-success

Narrowing the talent gap - Project Management Institute. Available at: https://www.pmi.org/learning/thought-leadership/narrowing-the-talent-gap

www.ingramcontent.com/pod-product-compliance
Lightning Source LLC
Chambersburg PA
CBHW070321220526
45465CB00013B/1984